Twenty One Of The Things I Don't Say

Valentina Nobile

Presentation by *BookLeaf Publishing*

Web: www.bookleafpub.com

E-mail: info@bookleafpub.com

ISBN: 9789357745031

First edition 2023

Past Self

Do you remember how you were?
Do you remember the things you used to say?
Do you remember how everyone could tell…
what you were going to do next?
Why have you changed?
Can you even recognize yourself?
You used to have such a bright light
you used to be the golden child.

I drown in your voices
I hear you even when you aren't around
Yes I remember
Yes I have changed
No I don't recognize myself
and I can tell that you already suspect

Memories don't help
Stop telling me to fix myself
You remembering won't make me change
I am still trying to forget that I was somewhere
else
My thoughts weren't even the same
There was no need for me to change
I didn't need to defy myself

A constant fight inside my mind
parts of myself that battle to stay intact
I am lost in my past self
in the crazy maze that is my head
stuck in a story with a written end
My predictable self wants to burn the pages of
my old self
I want to stop stressing over chapters I have
sworn to forget
"This isn't who you are" torments my nights
I don't want to think of it and forget with time
I am not there anymore
I am not a child anymore
I don't need guidance like I did before

Forgetting who I was is not the solution

I owe you sympathy past self
for I have neglected you when you helped me
build myself
You don't torment my nights
my country no longer haunts me at times
I am proud of how far I've come
You are doing great in a new home

Why should I feel guilty?
Why should I want to hide you in the past?
The future is right ahead
and I am preparing so it never chases me away

I have found peace in who I am
I have moved away, and I have left her behind
The girl she was would have never survived
poor girl, I remember now
I know who I was
I don't know how I ended up here, but I am glad
I did
for knowing how that girl was
I am afraid she would have never lasted

Can't you see I am here now?
I have come so far to cry now
I am waving from the other side
still the same underneath my skin
My past self handed me the ink
for me to write my way into who I am…
now that I am here.

Life Lesson

You know, I am a person of deep thoughts
I am used to feeling until I cannot stop
Once you say something, it is stuck
I cannot seem to let it go
the words fly around my mind
I could see them anywhere, even if I was blind
I try to not think of it
but how could I? I need it

I am also very strong
I was raised to be extremely tough
my mother taught me to do it all alone
there is no need to have you break my walls
If you say something hurtful again
I might just leave you and walk away
I don't need for you to stay
I have myself…
I can handle never seeing you again

But why is my heart shrinking?
Why the pain in my chest as I turn away?
Why am I attached to a burning flame?
I walk away, and it hurts
I get too close, and it burns
I was raised to be tough

So why can't I seem to let go?

You cloud my mornings with your tone
You ruin my mood when you are gone
Your sarcasm and your jokes
make me want to rip my skin off

You think it's so much fun
"it passes the time" you say as I cry
I am trying to tell you
I am begging you to understand
Why is it that I am trapped?
Why do you keep breaking my heart?

You keep asking me to stay
such a broken boy, please let me help
you tell me you won't be any good
I assure you I can handle all your moods

I tell you how I feel
I open up
and explain why I can't breathe
You hug me tight and kiss my forehead
"I just made a joke that went over your head"
and that's enough to make my heart drop once
again
you assure me nothing is wrong
but it was easy for you to leave me after all

"That is why I love you"
"I don't think I could ever leave you"
what a narcissistic liar
wanting to have me there because you were too
afraid of being left
your words hurt more than getting shot with a
gun
You don't know what love is
You don't make promises you cannot keep
You are a liar and a coward
I wish I had said that when I saw you after

You made me question myself
I started to hate myself
maybe I had done something wrong
maybe you needed me to do more

I can see that you are two-faced
but something about you feels like nothing else
I keep making up excuses
I keep looking away from the emotional bruises
I calm the voices in my head
I repeat to myself that it is not with bad intent
I want to make things right
I am sure it's just that no one has ever loved you
right

After seeing what you have turned into
I am embarrassed to have ever been with you

I don't regret it ever happening though
now I know what I am not looking for
I will never cry again laying on the floor
I won't reduce myself to ever being with a
broken boy
Your voice, your words
won't break me anymore
I have outgrown you
I simply wish you well
And I hope I never ever get to see you again.

When Our Eyes Close

I close my eyes and I see a world in color
no more shadows or monsters to haunt me at
night
but instead a beautiful bright light
it guides me through the darkest corridors of my
mind
showing me a world I had never seen before

The birds talk to me through their singing
telling me stories only they can tell
I see people I haven't seen before
people who don't even walk Earth anymore
I hear things no one has said
and read words that haven't been written before
I travel to different places
jumping from time to time
I can't separate fiction from reality
for my reality is more fantasy than it is real life

I remember things I hadn't thought about before
but as soon as I wake up they are all gone
memories and thoughts leave my mind
adventures I lived only last night
they fly away and disappear
for things aren't meant to last here

I was told to hold on
or else they'll leave
as if they had never even been—
a part of me before

We dream so we can follow the light
we dream cause we are mostly trapped inside
our minds
when we rest and turn it off
is when the most magical things come true
and one dream can mean something different—
people dream to go away
to let the imagination fly away

I close my eyes and choose to believe
that there is a world outside of what we can see
and when we all let ourselves rest
we will find each other wherever we go—
when dreams take over us all
as soon as our eyes close

My Person

Never thought I would ever get so lost
in such pretty eyes like the ones you own
your smile—your hair
give my lungs air
loving someone so deeply
being mesmerized by your laugh
I could go hours and hours
only listening to you rant
You're my favorite place on earth
my favorite person and safe place
you hold my heart in your hands
and I've never felt more secure and admired
Your hugs give me peace
and when your sweet lips touch mine
I feel as if the whole world was mine
My darling boy— my sweet love
how lucky I am to have found
my best friend in the most handsome man
people say it's wrong
to act as if you're my whole
but what they don't understand
is that my life had stopped
and the moment you walked through that door
I slowly began to realize
I no longer remember what it was like

to live each day without you in my life
my present and my future
are consumed with thoughts of you
for even though you're new
I feel as if I've known and loved every part of
you
way before the stories of our lives
had begun to come alive

Deadly Fears

I was once asked what my biggest fear was
I didn't know what to respond
I have never had a fear so strong
But now when I close my eyes
Even my heart made out of ice
trembles at the thought of that

I am standing all alone
there is no way back home
The darkness surrounding me hugs me tight
I find myself at a strange place
People looking at me wherever I went
no faces are even shown
I can't even recognize my own
But I feel like there is something I should know

I keep dreaming, and I dream big
I am just trying to be seen
The thought of being ordinary
hunts me like wolves hunt rabbits
I want to do something important
I want to be recognized
I don't want to pass away
and not even get flowers that day
I want my name to be remembered

I want tales written about myself
I don't want to fail
I don't want it all to be in vain

I say things without thinking
I can be mean and cruel
I don't want to hurt anybody
I don't want to be left alone
I am afraid I have no control over myself
I will react first and think later
then I won't stop thinking…
of what I could have done better

My mind haunts me at nights
Sometimes I can't even close my eyes
All the things I think about myself
there is a constant fight inside my head
I can really be against myself

I am afraid life is too short
So many things I won't be able to get done
and it's not being scared of when I die
but because I feel like I can't survive
There is so much going on
We are even killing our own world
No matter what I do
It can be game over soon

I want to live more

Why does life have to be so short?
I need to experience much more
But time is something you cannot control
I am constantly in autopilot mode
I need stimuli to make my brain work
I need adrenaline most of all
I need excitement to remember I am still not
gone
I don't want to be a part of the matrix
I want to be in control
I want to stop listening to "I told you so"

I get too close to people
When I care, I care too much
Why am I always getting so involved?
Once I am attached, I have no control
How do you want me to act?
Was I out of line?
I am trying to do everything right
I am not going to give you any reason
to want to leave me in this prison
I will always be there for you
I won't ask anything of you
but if you aren't there for me too
I will hold it against you
I expect to receive what I give
because every time I give
I lose a part of myself
I want to know if there is someone else

that can care as much as I intend

I can be fragile, and I hate it
I need attention, so pathetic
I need reassurance, so disgusting
I need validation, that's embarrassing
I am scared of being left, that's just great
abandonment issues are a real thing
But damn, why am I so intense?

Fear is who I am
I am afraid more than I am alive
Still, what marks the difference
Is that I embrace them…
I've never let them dictate who I am
because after all, when I look at myself
I fear a lot
but I will never let them make me stop

What It Means For Me To Love

There is nothing more beautiful than finding that perfect someone. That person that will be everything for you, and who you will be everything for. I am lost in the idea of being loved like that; so loved, it gets to when they want to be with you for life.
"For life", what an interesting choice of words. That can mean anything, things like life change so fast. We don't know anything. We don't know anything for sure, and nothing about life is certain. To have someone tell you that they want to have you for life, is the purest, simplest and most exciting proof of love ever. To build a home with the person that you want the most, to be able to share every morning, every kiss, every breath, every inch of that place with them…

Loving someone these days has turned into a fake feeling. We have destroyed the meaning of "love", and we have transformed it into a transaction. We have decided "If I give you this, you give me that." We have decided that picking someone, getting their hopes up for a couple of weeks and then dropping them is normal. We have decided that it is okay to tell someone that you love them, only to use them, leave them and get with someone else immediately. We have picked beautiful relationships, and destroyed them by calling them "situationships" because we are too afraid to commit to someone, or not mature enough to set our priorities straight. We kiss someone because we want to cross a new letter off of the alphabet for our "kiss list." We play with people's feelings, and we get involved for attention or validation to feed into our delusions and low self-esteem. We don't know what real love is like, and those who do, thank you for keeping it that way.

It is terrifying to think that this is what our children will experience. A love that doesn't fully love, a friend who you can't fully trust, a parent that doesn't fully take care of you, a relationship that isn't fully a relationship. It's embarrassing how mediocre we have become. How we can't even feel completely, and instead we allow ourselves to feel only to an extent. We have created boundaries and limitations for our feelings, and we lock them inside of ourselves before throwing away the key to let them out. We allow ourselves to love as far as the other one does. We stop ourselves from doing nice things for others because "would they do it, too?". We stop ourselves from loving because "what if they are cheating?" We stop ourselves from saying how we feel because "what if they leave me for it?"

I am tired of living with people that are too afraid to even live. I am tired of living with people who love halfway, or who romanticize abuse and toxic relationships. I crave pure love. I crave "I'll jump in front of a bus for you" people. I crave people that aren't afraid to feel and commit. I crave people who love and care and feel so intensely until their hearts feel like they will explode. I crave vulnerability and deep conversations. I crave talking about the future without fearing or overthinking. I crave reciprocity when it comes to honesty, commitment and respect and loyalty. I crave people, not robots who can control what they think, feel and how much they give. I want craziness. I want intensity. I want passion and fireworks.

I am not for this society. I am not for a halfway love. Live with me, die for me, go crazy with me, and let's get married. Let's do things right because there is beauty in it. Let me love you right without making me feel like "I am too much" or like "I am needy", and love me back

the same. Let me get consumed by you, and let
me burn with feelings because it is only then that
I will feel alive. Only then will I say that I truly
"love" someone.

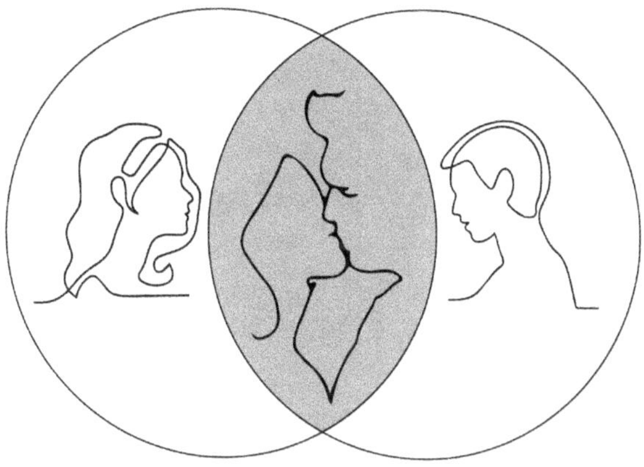

The Creep Inside My Mind

There is a creep inside my mind
the one that keeps on grabbing me tight
the one to blame for the tightness in my chest
the shaking of my hands
the cold sweat running down my face
the pressure on my lungs—
stopping the oxygen from allowing me
to breath in

I feel warm but I'm freezing from the inside out
there is light brightening the room but I can't see
past the dark
the shadows around me make me feel like
someone's watching

My chest is compressing my heart—
which hasn't stopped pumping so freaking fast
A million thoughts running through my mind
A million scenarios that are building up
there's tension all around me
panic in which I am drowning

I can't see past the negative thoughts
the overthinking and the anxiety

the glass looking half empty from where I am
standing
it's a panic room and I'm the only one locked
inside
with no clues to find
no escape from what I am feeling
not when I am the only one who can see it

I'm holding on with one hand
inches away from the edge
water running down my face
barely being held
by the anxiety that lives inside my head

It resides inside of me
playing with my worst fears
it reminds me every day
how much power it has over myself
and it holds me tightly and close
it's not planning on letting go
for it has become a part of who I am
the anxiety looks back at where I stand
reflecting the worst parts of who I am
it leaves me with permanent scars
and it creeps inside my mind
until it comes out and carves my skin out
and reminds me every day
how even after the good days

it will always come back to terrorize me during
the day
and keep me company once I lay in bed

To My Fellow Sisters

When I was a child… I never understood
Why can't I live however I want to?
Why can't I be whatever I want to be?
Why do I have to follow unacceptable rules?
How was I sent to live in a world where people
are now
killing their own?

I am a strong and independent person
So why am I being told to be scared of walking
alone?
Why should I try and cover myself up?
Why do I need to wear something more
"appropriate"
when male family members come to our home?
Why can't I be allowed to go out with only
guys?
Why can't I sleepover at my friend's because
there is a man
in the house?
Why am I being taught to be scared?
Why am I being taught to be scared of men?

Now… I understand

my sisters have experienced pain caused by men
I am lucky to have been saved
but how my heart aches for those who weren't
I will scream as if it happened to myself
I will stand with the mothers who lost their little
girls
And will pray for the soul of the girl that trusted
her guy best friends
But why should we be scared?
Why should we be taught to cover up?
Why should we be blamed for the horrendous
acts?
Why should we live with guilt and shame—
when all the abusers get a short penalty instead?

I am tired of being afraid
I don't want girls to cry without being heard
the abuser should be the one to blame
It is not our fault
We should be able to feel safe in the world
not scared of being alone
I don't want to be scared of all men
for it is not fair for those who are angels
but how can I tell girls
to walk freely in a world—
that already failed them

We are not toys you can play with
We are not a means to an end

women weren't made for men
and I will repeat that until I am dead!

You can't touch us if we don't want to
and you can't call us names when we reject you
grow up and learn to respect
don't force us into something we haven't
consent
stay the hell away from us and get some help

And for my sisters all around the world
I am so sorry you were there alone
I am so sorry no one heard you
I am so sorry he didn't respect you
You're not alone now
we all cry and stand by your side
for together we will work
to make the world heal once and for all

Self-Destructive Mind

I am my biggest enemy
I hurt myself with awful words
the villain inside my head
drowns my mind with thoughts about myself

Overthinking is like having
the evil version of yourself
creeping inside your head
it never shuts up
it never apologizes
it keeps on going until you accept
that maybe that is your fate

I will never stop thinking
I will never be able to shut down...
sometimes sleeping
is the best solution I can find

The voices in my head
keep wanting to make me fail
they act as if it's not enough
that my consciousness already–
torments me enough

Overthinking is like constantly falling

and floating over the deep void that is my head
it leaves me hanging while I scream for help
no one listens except for myself
I can tell they laugh at me
they think I am pathetic and weak
they give me the worst scenarios
they force me to think that I am not enough
they want me to agree with the horrible things
they say
they are powerful and sometimes they win
because they know how much control they have
over my self-destructive mind

Forever Friend

Friendship means different things
it's something that some people
might not even need
Others like myself
crave a special friend
a crazy one
one I cannot share
And I am lucky to be able to say
I have found one…
The one I will never forget
for I already met my forever friend

We were seven as we played
outside the house even during rainy days
you turned out to be my neighbor
how lucky am I to have met you

I remember when my sister asked if you wanted
to play
I remember being too ashamed
When you came running and said yes
I just knew that we would become best friends

We played for hours
We played for days

Suddenly it had been eight years
and we were still staying up late

You're the person with all my secrets
You're the one who saw me at my worst
You stood by my side and held my hand
You offered me support…
even when I proved to be absurd

From late afternoons riding a bike
Making promises and friendship pacts
To late nights crying and laughing
losing sleep but sharing dreams
To early mornings making breakfast
and you yelling at me
cause I always made a mess before we could eat
We sat on the kitchen floor and shared
the best of your pancakes
How I miss our talks…
actually, I might just miss your kitchen floor

No one matches my energy like you do
You understand me even better than I do
The best experiences I've had with you
I don't know what I would ever do without you

You'd fight me sometimes
We even pulled each other's hair until we cried
We laid in the middle of the road

What were we even fighting for?

I know you like no one else
I understand your craziness
Even in class, it would be the two of us
because we were too smart
for someone else to be in the same group with us

You're very intense
you're crazy and obsessed
you have very weird beliefs
and you always held me back like with a leash
Every time I was about to jump
you called me stupid and made me stop
you were always the responsible one
because if it had been for me
I think I would be nowhere to be seen

Thank you for holding me back
Thank you for always making me think twice
Now that we are apart
I am scared to fall apart
for you were the one keeping me together
you were the one with the rational decisions
I am standing at the edge
waiting for you to tell me to move away

You scare me half the time
and I'm always terrified to let you down

I admire you most of all
because you have such a unique soul

My forever friend… my sister for life
I will never be able to explain-
How grateful I am to have lived by your side
and the distance between us today
is just like the tiny wall
that separated us when we were young

I will forever be in debt to you
I will forever have your back
for you have been the greatest gift
that God gave me in life

Mrs. "I know it all"
Mrs. "I do it better than y'all"
Thank you for always being there
and for always listening to me complain
I am not the easiest person
I can be hard to love and care
I have had my own scars
but you never put me aside
Keep shining best friend
you will forever be the best person I've ever met

The Tamed Ones

Free spirits suffer the most
those we consider rebels
carry the scars of the world's voice
we, who go against the ordinary
become the outcasts of society

We see life from a different perspective
we stay away from black or white ideals
we choose to follow a different path
and we get looked down upon—
for wanting something other than that

Children of chaos are born to raise hell
we don't easily become afraid
we walk through fire and prevail
we are used to being looked at with disdain
we are at ease with the uncertain
and we find comfort in what hurts us
we take challenges and we want….
to do something different with our lives

I don't buy the idea that was given to me
the rules and norms of how my life should be
I don't want to live a life that has been planned

I want to be able to explore and experience
anything I want
I want to fall and get back up
I don't want to follow the conventional path
I won't settle for a life that has already been
lived
ages before I even got here

I like extraordinary things
I want to travel and learn new things
I don't want to feel trapped in this house
I don't want to feel trapped in my own life
I don't want a regular job
I don't care about money or having a wealthy
home
I don't want to work to live
but instead live so I can be free

I like chaos and disaster
that's how the most wonderful things happen
and even if we seek control
natural disasters will eventually blow it all
so I choose to follow the wind
I choose to work with what life gives me
I go against the conventional norms
because I am not a fucking toy

I won't let it all be under control
I don't want to follow steps on how to grow

there is a warrior inside of me
that will not let me go quietly
I am impulsive and strong
my character and thoughts feed my anger and—
it's burning my blood
so even if I wanted to….
I could not go a day being controlled—
like a kid playing with dolls

I have a wild heart
I find beauty in war
to me it shows that someone cares
enough to fight until death
I will refuse to close my eyes
and I haven't fully lost my sight
I won't follow the crowd
I won't be considered a sheep in someone's barn
my mother taught me to be a leader
"you gotta shine in a group of people"
and I intend on making her proud
even if my rebellion scares her at times

If you tell me to go right I will go left
if you tell me I am wrong I'll argue to prove I
am right
I won't ever turn down a challenge
and I will fight until I can't stand
for there is war running down my veins
there is an insatiable need to define myself

I prefer danger and uncertainty
than peace with an expiration date
So I choose to exist-
under my own damn terms
because why would I ever let the tamed ones
dictate how I should behave

Blank Page

I like to think of myself
as a story others will tell
I like to think of my body
as a blank page—
where I am able to document
my fascination for the secrets of the world
the words and the colors
the deepest meanings of things
the abstract things in life
and the things I can't even describe

My mind is the vessel for the new things I learn
I feed myself with knowledge
and I document it when I write
and when I see something I like
I want to engrave it for life
so all the tattoos on my skin
represent the most beautiful things—
the poems written on myself
the meaning of life itself
the dreams of a storyteller
the promises to my sister
the things I'll never be
and the things I wish to achieve
the art of my best friend
and the songs of the gods themselves

Little Sister

I was three when I first heard of you
One year later I finally met you
I was four the first time I held you
And when you smiled at me the first time
I knew we would be together for life

You had just been born
and struggles were already affecting us all
I saw you crying that one day
and I promised to myself
I would never let anything come your way

I knew what I had to do since then
I knew I'd always prioritize keeping you safe
you became my best friend
and I'd make sure to protect you any day

I will stand for what you choose to believe
I will always respect how you feel
And I will never let anyone disrespect you
Cause believe me if I say
I will be okay, if I end up going to jail
I will be loyal to you till the end
And I will always try to put a smile on that face

Dear sister… annoying little version of myself
I promise to always give you the world
and I cannot wait to see you grow
any moment when you are feeling down
I'll be here to cheer you up
and if someone ever makes you feel bad
I can assure you I can also handle that

I hope you never feel scared
I hope you know how much I truly care
You are the reason why it is hard to leave
I cannot think of ever wanting to leave you here

You are an extension of myself
you are going to be the better version of who I
am today
you will never have to worry about anything else
you will never have to worry about being by
yourself
wipe the tears away
if you ever feel like I am gone
Cause like the old saying tells…
"you are too well tangled around my soul"

Don't get it wrong though
I will snitch on you with mom
Please, don't mistake my loving words
for I will still not let you borrow my clothes
Yes, I love you like no one else

but to me, you still look like an elf

And so, my mini me
I will forever bother you
I will forever walk behind you
I will forever fight for you
I will forever choose you
But most of all
I will forever keep you close.

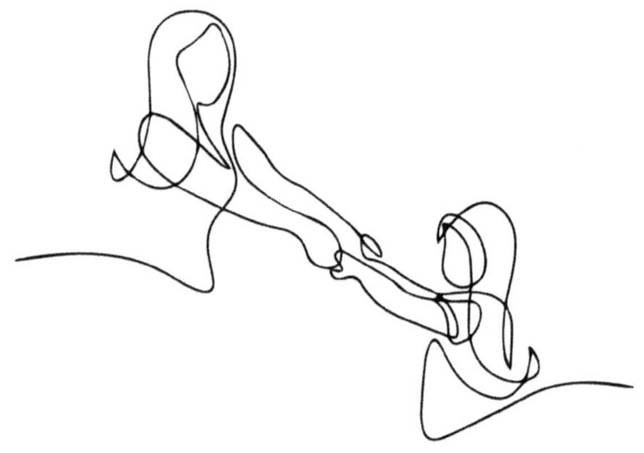

Memory Lane

As I open my eyes and wash my face
the cold water dripping down my hair
I look at myself in the mirror
and remind myself this is not a dream
I think about everything
as images and flashbacks run down my memory
lane
I smile as I sit back
and the nostalgic emotions come running at once
I've never felt more at peace
as I remember everything
and the realization hits
that memories are the purest thing
a person can hold on to and keep

Make It Stop

I feel so much at times
It comes all rushing like waves hitting the shore
at night
I run the opposite way
I promised to never let myself drown again
But when you look at me with those eyes
Ay Dios mio, what a beautiful sight…
After such pain, one changes with no regret
but when you meet someone extraordinary,
the heart melts like once iced water.
The emotions that overwhelm me, become the
ones
I crave the most.
I feel so much at times. I feel until the sky runs
out of stars,
one for each emotion that crosses my heart.
I love and I care deeply; but, once it's gone,
there is no single soul
that will bring the feeling back.
I am the sweetest and coldest person one can
meet.
I am either a daydream or a nightmare come
true.
I wish it wasn't like that. I wish I wasn't always
so black or white.

When I care, you could get me to take a bullet
for you; but, when I don't,
I could make you feel as if you weren't even
real.
If you wronged me, then you deserve it, but how
do I make it stop when I have simply turned it
off?
How do I make it stop when it happens because
you didn't look at me long enough?
How do I make it stop when it happens because
you didn't sound excited when you texted me
"hello"?
How do I make it stop when it happens because
you were too busy to respond?
How do I make it stop when it happens because
I overthink and assume the worst?
How do I make it stop when the real villain is
myself and not someone else?
How do I make it fair? How do I get myself to
feel again?
I turn my emotions off, and it's such a scary
thing; to love and admire, and suddenly detach
and completely delete someone off my mind.
I am afraid of how cold I can get. I am afraid of
losing someone who cares because I can't
control my emotions well. I feel intensely until
it's gone; and once it's gone, then I go numb.

Mami

To my mother, the strongest person ever
I am who I am because you were who you were
I owe most of my victories to you, and I know
you'll say it was all me; but, truth is
you had everything to do with the things I have
achieved.
Through mistakes and effort
stress and sweat
long nights staying up–
and early morning waking up before the sun
came out
Through love and affection
homemade food and warm hugs
boundaries and screams
laughing out loud until the neighbors called the
police
endless support and admiration…
You have raised me to be myself
and also carry the part of yourself
that you and I both—
admire and appreciate the most.
Thank you, mami, for the sacrifices you made
for loving me even when I was annoying
for staying by my side even when I had lost my
mind

for clearing the path to my current life
for giving me a strong mind
and a wild heart
for being my hero and my worst enemy at times
and for showing me kindness while I make sure
to speak my mind
for showing me how to be respectful and love
others
but most of all…
for giving me a family and a beautiful home.

La Arena En El Mar

When I met you I didn't know
how deeply I would fall in love
I'd cross oceans and fight dragons
I'd run from country to country
only to find you

Because finding you isn't like having just met
you
but like finally remembering the word that had
been at the top of your tongue for a whole day
long
It's like listening to a song and knowing you will
be listening to it nonstop
and finding you is like walking into a room full
of art
finding you is like getting a deja-vu from our
past life

You're the most familiar nonmemory I have
The closest I've ever felt to traveling in time
You're the newest yet oldest friend of mine
and loving you is as if I've loved you all my life

Every time I touch your skin, I remember the
feeling of electricity in myself…

and when I trace your lips with my finger
my mind is invaded with flashbacks and
memories
all the places you have kissed, the sweet things
you whisper to my ear
and the warm feeling of your touch every time
you pull me close

You're too tangled around my soul,
like ink tattooed on my skin
and every night my heart cries
it aches when you aren't around
it remembers the everlasting feeling of the nights
sleeping skin to skin
as you held me tightly closer to your chest

Closing my eyes and feeling such peace
an overwhelming feeling that it is here where I
want to be
I am yours every day, my love
I am vulnerable with you and I choose
to give you all of me
for you're the person that stormed in my heart
as if it had never even been mine
and I let you in and make a mess
because it's still you who it beats for anyway

anyone that isn't you
disappears from my view

for you took everyone's place
you came and conquered as you planned to stay
everyone else became irrelevant
no one's ever gotten close to the feelings you
make me feel

I love you...
but those three words aren't enough anymore
so let me put it in a way that is easier to
understand
in the language I love and want you to learn
Te amo...
más que toda la arena que hay en el mar,
y más que el universo de estrellas en la noche
más estrellada en nuestra tierra.

Jealously

My heart burns red
heated flames grow instead
I don't want to share...
what is mine, mine stays
don't tell me it is fine
it won't be until you are in my arms

Possessiveness describes who I am
what a hideous trait to have
but emotions can't always be controlled
so when I am jealous my face says it all
it is impossible to hide
so eventually everyone finds out

Jealousy comes from insecurity
or so they say…
but I don't worry about those things
all I want is to be the one thing you see
Make me your one and only
show me how you feel
make sure we are on the same page
or else, I'll go insane

I wish it wasn't like that
I wish I could remain calm

but I don't want anyone to touch what is mine
if you are available then you aren't on my side
I burn in rage
but I will never show
for thank god the one thing I can control
is my pride before it all

It feels as if that's all I can think of
thoughts and dangerous opinions
if I feel like I am not respected
I will leave without any questions
It isn't a good thing
I am aware and I'm able to admit it
but how can I control–
a human mistake that is already in my blood.

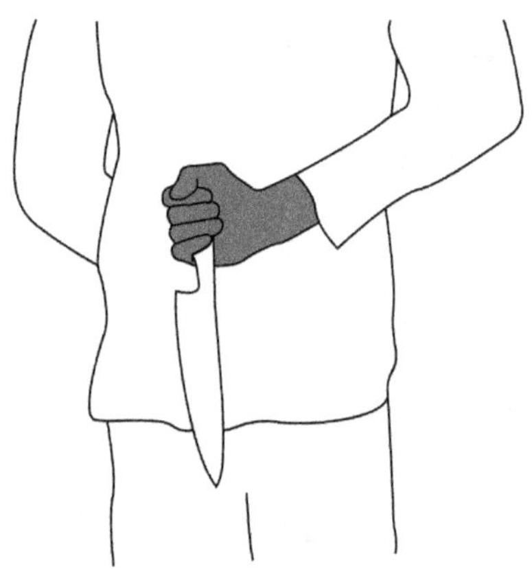

Healing

Everybody wants you to be okay
everybody is always wishing you the best
"Get better" they say
"I hope you are happy again" those words are
stuck in my head

it needs to get bad so it can all be fine
the healing process sometimes—
hurts more than what originally made you sad

When nothing feels right
and you can't help but not want to go out
you find comfort in the pain
in the numbness that comes when you are
depressed
So how do you warm up to the idea of being
okay again?
How do you find yourself after being lost for so
long?

Opening your heart to growth
allowing happiness to come inside your home
accepting defeat and being patient
letting your mind rest
while you build yourself once again

letting go of the sadness
forcing yourself to get up every day
not letting the world consume you
being kind to yourself
accepting the love you deserve
moving on from the memories
letting all hopes go
forgiving yourself for letting you fall into a deep
hole
Letting the scars heal without being hunted by
the guilt of moving on
because sometimes the only thing we remain
attached to
is the knife pressed against our heart
that keeps making us bleed and cry
but healing as we start letting go…
dropping the knife seems like the biggest failure
of all

Be kind and patient
it does get better
but first remember—
it will rain first
so the rainbow can come after the storm

To My Little Friend

Home can be multiple places and home can be
multiple people
For me the meaning of it is simple because it's
one little friend that makes everything peaceful.
Life can be hard, and it is even worse when you
deal with it alone,
but you are the light at the end of the tunnel.
You are the one that makes life more enjoyable.
You make it easy for me to be myself because
you never asked for me to change.
Friendship means different things for people.
For some it can be something ephemeral… and
for others a necessity to survive loneliness.
I don't want you when I am alone,
instead I want to share with you the moments I
enjoy the most.
When I am with multiple people and having fun,
it is you who I wish was here
to share it with me.
My best friend and twin flame, I am certain that
we will last an eternity.
I am tired of having to find a special person after
a little while.
I am happy with you. I wouldn't want anyone
other than you.

I have fallen in love with our friendship, with
our memories and our laughs.
Nothing brings me more joy than crying because
of how funny we are.
Every moment with you is precious, and finding
myself in someone else is something I never
thought I would have…
cause I think I am out of my head, but turns out
you're also out of your mind.
When I met you, I never imagined that you
would be just like me.
I remember our first conversations, our first
photos together and the first time we went out.
I remember how nervous I was, cause I have
been hurt before
and it was scary to be vulnerable once again.
Turns out you were a miracle. The missing piece
to my puzzle.
The greatest adventure of it all and my best
friend for life.
I want to see us grow old together. I want to see
where life takes us.
I want to tell you "I told you so" when you are
the first one to get wrinkles when we are old.
I want to celebrate good news with you, and cry
next to you when we get hurt.
I want to travel with you and go on many dates,
as we try different restaurants but still eat a plain
burger.

I want to gain and lose friends, while you and I
stay the same.
I want to make jokes and create new phrases that
no one else understands.
I want to keep getting two hours early to work
just so we gossip like we haven't already before.
I want to go to different places and get shots
wherever we go.
You are my other half, the shadow to my soul
and the twin star that follows me around.
We are a team and the best one of all.
I will forever support you even if you tell me the
craziest thing ever.
You are my home and safe place. I will never let
anyone break us apart.
I will never let you down, and I will protect our
friendship with my life.
You are the one person that will always stand by
me,
and I promise to fight anyone for you because I
know you trust me to take care of it.
Thank you for picking me, I don't know what I
did to deserve this.
You are so special and kind-hearted, so talented
and smart. I will forever make sure everybody
else sees that.
My best friend and platonic love, I love you
today and I'll be sure to find you in our next life,
too.

I Am A Writer

I am a writer
I write until I have nothing left to say
but the thing about myself
is that I always have a story to tell

I write because that is who I am
If I am not writing then I suffocate with thoughts
I create stories that have never been told
stories that my mind tells my soul

The characters that live inside my mind
fighting to be a part of my next line
they hold the secret parts of myself
that I am too afraid to let escape

I write because that is how I speak
I write because it allows me to breath
I write because it is powerful
and it lets me speak a little louder
I write because all the voices in my head
never stop telling me to use my words…
to do something for the world

I am a writer— I am a poet
I own adventures and stories

I listen to the silence
and I make stories out of the quiet
I speak my truth when I write
and the pages that aren't blank
hold what I wish I could say out loud

I write because I drown in my thoughts
I can't find a way to let them go
but once I write and put those words down
I read and understand
what my soul couldn't find a way to explain

I can be quiet and I am observant
I watch and I analyze
I study people and expressions
so I can give my characters adventures
I keep them alive with what I see
that I later write before going to sleep

I live in my own little world
the world I created for the people that I love
I feel at ease with my imagination
I am able to find myself in each creation
I write about what I love
I write about people I am not
They represent the parts of myself that I hide
the parts that sleep deep inside
The ink on my pages sets them free
because how selfish of me would it be

to not find them a place to live

I am not what I write
I am the coward that hides behind the lines
I build these stories so I can feel
like I am more than what everyone else sees
I am not my characters
but they are some parts of who I am
they represent who I want to be
living the extraordinary life I wish I could live

I write about what hurts
I don't cry or let myself hurt
I am a writer and it's my job
to use the pain to create wonders and love
I feed my stories with horror
I take away what my characters mostly crave
I bleed on my pages
to let the world trapped inside myself be free
and to let the character, the reader and the writer
in me
find their right place to be

Writing mends the broken parts
writing builds hope and makes me feel alive
I write because I want others to feel
fascination for the world only I can see

Finally, I write…
I write simply because I am alive
I write because it is in my veins
to scream as I shatter the limitations life has to
offer…
for in my books and in my stories
there are no boundaries that can stop me
I'll play all the roles I create
and I will prevail
for life is ephemeral
but my words are now marked
and cannot be removed from the hard stone I
have carved.

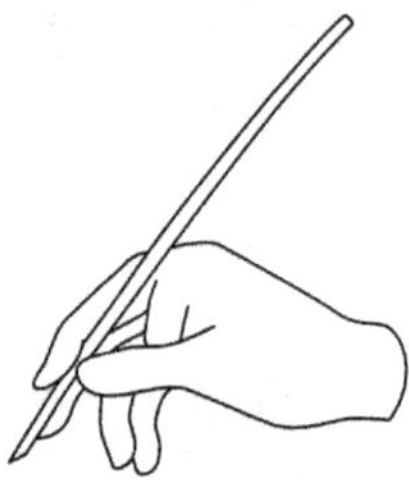